Original title:
Riddles in the Redwoods

Copyright © 2025 Creative Arts Management OÜ
All rights reserved.

Author: Fiona Harrington
ISBN HARDBACK: 978-1-80567-196-1
ISBN PAPERBACK: 978-1-80567-495-5

Whispers Beneath the Canopy

In the forest, secrets play,
Trees giggle as squirrels sway.
Roots twist with stories to share,
Leaves rustle without a care.

Chirps and caws begin to tease,
Beneath the boughs, there's mischief, please!
What hides behind that thick old trunk?
A rabbit's tale or a raccoon's punk?

Secrets of the Ancient Grove

Whispers drift on breezy nights,
Under stars that shine so bright.
What did the owl say to the bat?
"Let's play dress-up; how about that?"

Mossy carpets hide the truth,
Sprightly giggles betray our youth.
Who carved the hearts in bark so high?
A lovesick bee or a clever fly?

Enigmas Among the Giants

Tall trunks wear hats of misty hue,
Shake their branches, they'll giggle too.
What's the trick behind the bark?
A tree with jokes—let's leave a mark!

Among the shadows, mysteries bloom,
With laughter that dispels the gloom.
What's wiggly, furry, and loves to hide?
A secret squirrel on a thrilling ride!

Mysteries Etched in Bark

In grooves and lines, the stories hide,
Of moonlit dances and the tide.
What did the raccoon forget today?
A hat or snacks, oh what a fray!

Crickets serenade a playful scene,
As shadows stretch where the trees convene.
Why do the branches sway and bend?
To catch a joke from a feathered friend!

The Enigma of the Twisted Trunks

In a grove where trees all mumble,
A squirrel jokes, making us stumble.
With knotted roots that twist and bend,
They've secrets we can never send.

The branches sway, they start to lean,
What do they hide? Oh, what a scene!
A humor that wraps 'round the bark,
Their punchlines echo in the dark.

The Forest's Hidden Lexicon

Whispers dance like leaves in flight,
Words fall down, oh what a sight!
A fox explains with cheeky grace,
His vocabulary's quite the chase.

Beneath each frown and playful glance,
A story hides, inviting us to dance.
The trees all laugh, they shake their leaves,
A comedy in nature weaves.

The Dance of the Dappled Sun

Sunbeams skip on the forest floor,
Lighting up smiles and opening doors.
They play hide and seek in patchy light,
While giggles echo, taking flight.

The shadows join with a playful leap,
In this merry dance, secrets keep.
As critters sway to the sun's soft tune,
Nature chuckles, afternoon in bloom.

Charms of the Canopy

Look up high, the branches jest,
Swinging low, trying their best.
With every twist, they pull a prank,
A tangled joke, the forest's prank.

They twirl and swirl in leafy cheer,
A chorus of laughter fills the sphere.
The secrets up high will soon reveal,
The charm that makes the forest feel.

Lurking Legends in the Foliage

In shadows where the squirrels chat,
A ghostly figure dons a hat.
"Why do trees wear coats of green?"
"To look good, of course, they're so keen!"

Behind each bark, a mystery lies,
Who tickles the branches? Oh, what a surprise!
"Why do leaves hug the ground so tight?"
"They're just afraid of a windy night!"

Twilight Queries of the Twilight Grove

At dusk, the owls ponder and stare,
"Why does the moon always have flair?"
"Is it true that stars are just fireflies?"
"They've got their own gig in the skies!"

Beneath the glow of the silver light,
A band of raccoons plots for a bite.
"Why steal treasure from a picnic basket?"
"Because we're both thieves and quite the rascal!"

Whispers Among the Giants

In the grove where secrets loom,
The trees gossip of impending doom.
"Why do we stand so tall and proud?"
"To see over the heads of the crowd!"

A little chipmunk twitches its tail,
"Why do we tell such silly tales?"
"To make the wind laugh, that's why!"
"And who knew trees could sigh?"

Secrets Beneath the Canopy

Underneath where the shadows dance,
Mushrooms giggle, given a chance.
"What's the best joke in the forest floor?"
"Knock, knock! Who's there? Fern, and nothing more!"

Roots weave tales of old and new,
"Why do they intertwine, it's true?"
"To hold hands tight and not let go!"
"Friendship's the best that we know!"

The Intrigue of Intertwined Vines

A vine once whispered, "Can you see?"
It twisted and turned, just like me.
Climbing up high, a daring spree,
But tripped on a branch, oh what a plea!

In the canopy, shadows play,
Giggles echo in a leafy ballet.
Roots entwined, they join the fray,
Who's winning this gamesome display?

With tendrils grasping, a sly embrace,
They crafted a game, a leafy race.
"Catch me if you can," left no trace,
An acorn rolls by, a comedic chase!

In this jungle where laughter reigns,
The silly vine sways, ignoring pains.
Tangled in jest, what fun remains,
A dance of delight, no real strains!

Messages of the Mysterious Moss

Soft as a pillow, the moss did grin,
"I overheard secrets, let me begin!"
Whispers of squirrels, and giggling kin,
Playing hide and seek in the forest's din.

Like fuzzy green carpets, they spread out wide,
"Come and sit down, I'll be your guide!"
With tales of the trees, in shadows they hide,
Come gather around, let's enjoy the ride.

Spongy and giggly, it tickled toes,
Sharing odd rumors of tall, creeping crows.
"They wear silly hats!" the moss surely knows,
In this woodland chat, laughter just flows.

So, heed these soft words where jokes unfold,
Spread like the moss, let your stories be told.
In this forest of fables, be brave, be bold,
For messages shared are pure gold!

Wonders in the Woodland

In a glade of giggles, the tall trees sway,
Whispering tales in a merry display.
Where squirrels parade in their nutty ballet,
And badgers debate the best game to play.

The ferns throw shade, like a room so cool,
While chipmunks chatter, "Who's the biggest fool?"
They flip and they tumble, breaking the rule,
Laughing and dancing, no time to stool.

Mushrooms wear spots like a whimsical hat,
"Have you tried jumping?" cried the curious cat.
With each little leap, they got lost in that,
The woodland's a circus, imagine that!

So come join the fun, where the wild things are,
Under the twinkling, amazing stars.
Each moment unique, like a gift from afar,
Life here is a giggle, not a memoir!

The Labyrinth of Leafy Veils

A maze of green with twists and bends,
Where shadows twirl and light descends.
"Which way to go?" ask flustered friends,
Each path leads to laughter that never ends.

With ferns that tickle and branches that sway,
They playfully giggle, come join the fray.
Elusive pathways that lead you astray,
In the woods, it's a game – come out and play!

A wise old owl hoots, "What a crazy sight!"
Mice wear sunglasses, all dressed up tight.
With chatter and chuckles, they take flight,
In a leafy labyrinth, pure delight!

So hop through the maze, no need for a guide,
Embrace the confusion, let laughter slide.
Amid the green whispers, joy won't hide,
In the heart of the woods, let fun be your tide!

The Enchanted Understory

Underneath the leafy green,
Squirrels dance in glee, unseen.
Who knew that acorns could bring cheer?
Their tiny giggles, loud and clear?

Mushrooms sport their polka dots,
Claiming space in quirky spots.
The trees are gossiping today,
About the ants and their ballet.

A rabbit lost his lucky sock,
Blaming it on a tick-tock clock.
With laughter bubbling all around,
Nature's joy is truly found!

So wander through this playful maze,
Where creatures share their silly ways.
Each whispered secret, delight unwrapped,
In this woodlands' space, all are entrapped.

Secrets of the Sun-Dappled

In the patch where sunlight falls,
Chirps rise up like little calls.
A ladybug wearing a crown,
Claims the throne but wears a frown.

The shadows play their sneaky game,
Hiding laughter, never the same.
A wily fox with a tail so grand,
Picks up clues across the land.

With petals drifting like lost dreams,
The flowers giggle, burst at the seams.
"Guess my color!" one boldly shouts,
While butterflies dance all about.

So stroll beneath this playful glow,
Follow the whispers, let your heart flow.
In this sun-dappled realm, full of cheer,
Adventures await, just draw near.

A Symphony of Shadows

In the whispering evening breeze,
Balletic shadows twist with ease.
A raccoon strums a leafy tune,
While crickets chirp 'neath the moon.

The owls wear spectacles, quite proud,
Reading books to an unseen crowd.
'Tell a joke,' they hoot with glee,
While foxes laugh 'neath their leafy tree.

Acorns roll like marbles round,
As chipmunks race to claim their ground.
"Who's the fastest?" the shadows tease,
In this natural playhouse, everyone agrees.

As night drapes a silky cape,
The trees form a dynamic shape.
Each secret shared, a spark of delight,
In this symphony of shadows, taking flight.

The Woodlands' Whispers

In the woods, where shadows creep,
Trees tell stories, warm and deep.
A squirrel thinks he holds the key,
To a treasure beneath the old pine tree.

A chipmunk naps with a tiny grin,
Dreaming of the joy within.
"What's the best nut?" he loudly calls,
As laughter echoes off the walls.

The breeze carries a giggle and tease,
Nature's laughter dances with ease.
"Guess where I hid all my acorn stash!"
Each critter joins for a fun-filled bash.

As twilight paints the world in glow,
Whispers merge, a jovial flow.
In this woodlands, treasures delight,
With every chuckle, day turns to night.

Dreams in the Dense Forest

In shadows deep, the critters creep,
Squirrels plot, while bullfrogs leap.
An owl hoots, saying, "Who, oh who?"
While chipmunks giggle, it's all a zoo!

A raccoon wears a hat so tall,
He stumbles 'round, he's bound to fall.
But laughter fills the leafy space,
As the forest dances, in silly grace!

A fox in socks, what a sight to see,
He juggles acorns beneath a tree.
The mushrooms chuckle, a merry bunch,
Join the party, it's time to crunch!

Amid the pines, the humor flows,
With each twist, a mystery grows.
In dreams alive, the forest sings,
Of whimsical paths and funny things.

Trails of Twilight

As twilight drapes the silent trees,
The critters gather, doing as they please.
With fireflies twinkling like stars on a string,
A wise old turtle shares tales of spring.

A rabbit hops in oversized shoes,
While the bird in the bush sings bluesy blues.
The shadows snicker behind every trunk,
As the bushes sway, infused with funk.

The beetles march with a tap-tap beat,
While the raccoon dances with two left feet.
Beneath the moon, they sway and twirl,
In trails of twilight, let the fun unfurl!

Oh, speak to the owls, they're wise and sly,
With riddles that make you laugh and cry.
In this woodland realm, joy takes its flight,
A nightly party, till morning light!

A Tale of Twisted Branches

In tangled limbs where laughter grows,
A squirrel tells tales that nobody knows.
With acorns that bounce and giggles galore,
Each twist of the branch opens a door.

The raccoon wears spectacles, looking quite quaint,
While a chatty parrot tries to paint.
With colors so bright, it's a glorious mess,
Even the tree trunks are dressed to impress!

The frogs on a lily pad throw a grand fête,
With crickets strumming till very late.
"Why did the tree break up?" they quip with glee,
"Because it couldn't find a true root to be!"

In shadows capering, the night plays on,
With giggles echoing till the dawn.
In twisted branches, joy finds its way,
In this leafy realm, where we all play!

The Forest's Muffled Murmurs

The trees are chatting, whispers abound,
As breezes carry secrets all around.
A snail recites poetry, slow and precise,
While the bears giggle, not thinking twice.

"Why didn't the pine tree date a spruce?"
"Because she couldn't handle his massive juice!"
In muffled murmurs, the stories grow,
Of high-flying dreams and friends below.

The nightingale croons with a wink of delight,
Under starry skies, a jolly sight.
A hedgehog chuckles, "Oh, what a stew,
We're all misfits here, but we'll make do!"

In laughter's embrace, the forest reveals,
A kingdom of joy, that spins on wheels.
Each rustle and giggle, a story so bright,
In the heart of the woods, where dreams take flight.

The Quest of the Quiet Grove

In a forest quite deep, where the shadows play,
A squirrel with a hat thinks he's lost his way.
He asks for directions from a wise old tree,
But the tree just laughs, 'It's a mystery to me.'

A raccoon nearby, with a twinkle of glee,
Claims he found some treasure, come take a look, see!
He digs through the leaves, but it's just a shoe,
Now the squirrel's confused, and the tree's chuckling too.

The sun starts to set, casting shadows so strange,
And the animals gather, no need for a change.
With laughter they bond in this silly old place,
In the heart of the grove, life finds its own pace.

So if you venture forth to the quietest glade,
Listen for giggles that the forest has made.
For a quest here is fun, full of quirky surprise,
Even tall trees join in, with their long, leafy sighs.

Clues in the Canopy

A parrot was squawking, 'I've got a big clue!'
But all of his secrets seem lost in the blue.
He flutters and flaps above branches so high,
While a monkey just munches on fruit, oh my my!

'What's the great mystery?' the monkey does ask,
To which the parrot replies, 'That's a tricky task!'
He squints with one eye, and he tilts to the side,
While the monkey just giggles, unable to hide.

They look for a puzzle, or perhaps some delight,
In the tangled-up roots, where the shadows invite.
'There's magic in silence, and wisdom from wings,'
Squeals the fox from below, as he dances and sings.

So come join the fun, where the branches embrace,
In the canopy laughs, there's a whimsical space.
With creatures of all kinds, it's a festive parade,
Where the search for a clue turns to plans that they've made.

Oaths of the Old Timber

Old timber stands tall, with stories to tell,
As owls gather nearby, casting shadowy spells.
They vow 'til the dawn, we'll guard this grand space,
And in whispers share tales of the past they embrace.

A badger pops out from his hidden nook,
'You can't keep a secret if no one will look!'
With a wink and a grin, he stirs up some cheer,
And the old trees chuckle, for wisdom's quite near.

They pledge to protect every bird and each bee,
And vow to host parties beneath their grand canopy.
A wild dance erupts, under moon's silver light,
With creatures rejoicing, it's a magical night!

So raise up a toast to the ancient and wise,
In the oaths that they make, with mischief-filled eyes.
For in every echo of laughter and song,
The old timber whispers, 'Together we belong!'

Conversations with the Wind

The wind likes to chat with the leaves as they sway,
Telling jokes about clouds that wander astray.
'Why did the rain drop? It just wanted to play!'
Leaves giggle and rustle; they dance in the fray.

A fox pricks his ears, hears the stories anew,
'Tell me, dear wind, is the sky really blue?'
'It's a frame made of dreams, a trick of the eye,
Just like the tall tales that the stars tell at night!'

With whispers of secrets, the breeze carries on,
As squirrels share gags of the world they hop on.
'What if the sun wore a hat and some shoes?'
The wind just laughs, 'Oh, those are good views!'

So if you find stillness, and silence around,
Listen closely for laughter, where joy can be found.
For the wind's always chatting, with whimsy to lend,
In the world that surrounds us, where roots twist and bend.

Puzzles of the Pine Cones

Beneath the boughs, oh so wide,
Pine cones giggle, trying to hide.
They roll and tumble with great delight,
Making squirrels dance in the light.

Each pine cone boasts a secret tale,
Of woodland critters who set sail.
With a wink and a nod, they play a trick,
Saying, "Count us all, but choose quick!"

A sneaky breeze whispers through trees,
As pine cones chuckle in the tease.
They drop like raindrops, what a sight!
Who knew conifers had such a bite?

So gather 'round, let the games unfold,
With giggling cones, so brave and bold.
In this forest, humor is free,
Join the fun, oh come see me!

Echoes in the Evergreen

In the shade where the tall ones sway,
Echoes bounce and frolic all day.
Branches quirk, their voices blend,
Mischief waits around each bend.

A silly crow takes center stage,
Reciting lines from a birdie page.
The trees reply with a rustling cheer,
Laughter dances, so crystal clear.

Mossy floors oracles play,
Drawn in circles, come what may.
"Why did the squirrel cross the stream?"
"His acorn stash was but a dream!"

With every chuckle, the forest beams,
Tales unfold like magical dreams.
In greenery deep, where fun is found,
The echoes of joy lift off the ground!

Hidden Paths in the Forest

In the thicket where shadows squeak,
Lies a path that is truly unique.
Follow the trail of giggles and grins,
Where secret jokes ignite the spins.

A fox stands guard, with a cheeky grin,
"Enter here, if you dare, let the games begin!"
The branches rustle, whispers grow,
Who knows where this silly path will go?

Beneath the leaves, a rabbit hops,
Around him, the laughter never stops.
"What's under the hat," he slyly asks,
"Just your own wit—now that's a task!"

So wander on, don't be afraid,
In the hidden paths where the fun is made.
The forest swirls with giggles and glee,
In its embrace, forever you'll be!

The Conundrum of the Canopy

High above where the branches meet,
A puzzling game unfolds, oh what a treat.
Leaves whisper secrets, a playful affair,
Can you solve them, if you dare?

The acorn council gathers sly,
Debating who can touch the sky.
"Is it the bird, or maybe a breeze?"
They all burst out laughing, if you please!

A dance of shadows and sunlight plays,
Creating riddles through sunlit rays.
"Why's the tree so tall?" they chime,
"Because it knew that it's tree-mendous time!"

So climb the tales woven high,
In the canopy's arms, let laughter fly.
With every turn, a new delight,
In this puzzling wood, all feels just right!

The Leaf's Silent Syllogism

In the forest, leaves debate,
About their fate and the trees' weight.
One leaf claims it's quite a shame,
The others laugh, it's all a game.

A squirrel jumps in, tail aflame,
"This isn't logic, it's just plain lame!"
But they all giggle under the sun,
While nature's pulse makes the fun run.

The wise old bark begins to chime,
"What's logic without a little rhyme?"
So the leaves dance in swirling flight,
Creating riddles that feel just right.

Laughter floats through the swaying trees,
As each leaf crinkles in gentle breeze.
The forest holds secrets, sure and sly,
But laughter shared will always comply.

Petals of Paradox

A flower wondered why it turned bright,
When it opened wide to morning light.
"Am I the sun or just a blur?"
The bee buzzed back, "You're such a spur!"

Petals whisper secrets, soft and sly,
"Is it the land, or are we the sky?"
Every color boasts, every shade sings,
In a world where fun is the finest of things.

Daisies dance with dandelion dreams,
They plot and giggle in flowing streams.
"What if we're all just here to jest?"
They ponder aloud, feeling quite blessed.

A violet chuckles, "Oh, can't you see?
Our blooms are jokes of allergy!"
And the garden roars with delightful glee,
Petals of paradox, wild and free.

The Great Bark Conspiracy

In the grove, a whisper took flight,
Bark buddies huddled, deep in the night.
"We're the sentinels, let's scheme and plot,"
A beech bark proclaimed, with mischief caught.

Each bark joined in, a bark bandit crew,
Tell secrets of squirrels and owls that flew.
"So, here's the plan, let's have some fun,
We'll trick the forest before we're done!"

Pine needles laughed, snug on their beds,
"Let's paint up this place with colors and threads!"
With laughter and giggles, trees helped disguise,
Sticks wore bright hats; what a bold surprise!

As dawn broke, laughter rang true and wide,
The trees were all dressed, with bushy pride.
"Those tourists will think it's an art fair!"
The bark buddies chuckled, without a care.

Elysian Queries of the Wildwood

In the wildwood, questions flew free,
"Do mushrooms talk? Can acorns see?"
An owl hooted, pondering away,
"Could trees be dreaming while we play?"

Bunnies twitched, with a wink and a nod,
"Let's ask the daisies, they've surely trod!"
With whispers of wonder, they huddled tight,
"Let's solve the puzzle before it's night."

A frog croaked loudly, "Hold out your hands,
Let's catch some mysteries—where do they land?"
And the leaves rustled, giggles turned wild,
As nature conspired, each creature beguiled.

"Can we count the stars on the bark's rough skin?
Or does the moon play tricks, making us grin?"
These questions swirled through the twilight haze,
In the wildwood's charm, laughter always stays.

Responses of the Forgotten Timber

In the forest where shadows play,
A tree once spoke in a funny way.
"What's green outside yet brown within?"
With laughter, the squirrels grinned.

A log rolled over, thought it was slick,
"What's made of wood but isn't a stick?"
The birds just chirped, fluffed up their feathers,
While the old owl hooted, "It's me, of course!"

A breeze rustled leaves for a riddle delight,
"What goes up but never takes flight?"
The pinecones giggled, so round and spry,
"Your guess is as good as a cloud in the sky!"

Thus echoes the laughter from tree to tree,
Secretive whispers, as fun as can be.
In the deep of the woods, where secrets blend,
Come listen close, let the laughter suspend!

Tangles of Time and Truth

In the thicket, the vines intertwine,
They joke about keeping secrets divine.
"What can you hold without a grasp?"
The branches chuckled, it's hard to clasp.

An acorn dropped with a curious thud,
"What's born in spring, yet sleeps in the mud?"
The ferns twirled in laughter so wild,
"It's a memory that nature has compiled!"

Roots shared tales of an ancient spree,
"What has no legs but runs like a spree?"
The wind piped up with a whimsical hum,
"It's gossip we share, swirling like drum!"

Amidst the laughter, riddles bloom bright,
In the tangles of time, the truth takes flight.
Nature's jesters, the trees and the ground,
A funny refrain where joy can be found.

Sylvan Stonehouse Secrets

Under the canopy, stones start to chat,
"What runs but isn't a marathon brat?"
Moss giggled softly, rolling with glee,
"It's a river's secret, just flow and be free!"

In the shadows where memories dwell,
"What's light as a feather, can tell but not yell?"
The mushrooms pranced, their caps in a swirl,
"It's a secret kept in the soft, dark curl!"

The stones piled high, chuckled round and stout,
"What builds up strength, but does not shout?"
The leaves whispered back, in rustling tones,
"It's wisdom collected, in timeless stones!"

Secrets of the sylvan, in mirth entwined,
With laughter and riddles, they've gently aligned.
The forest's humor, a whimsical thought,
In the stonehouse of secrets, joy is sought!

Ghosts of the Great Canopy

Way up high where the old ghosts play,
They tickle the branches in a ghostly sway.
"What has no eyes but can still see?"
The leaves trembled softly, 'Tis a mystery!

A wisp of wind with a chuckle flew by,
"What's invisible, yet fills the sky?"
The shadows laughed, weaving in light,
"It's the jokes of the night that take flight!"

Among the treetops, giggles abound,
"What's light as air, yet makes no sound?"
The echoes whirled like a phantom dance,
"It's the humor of silence, if you take a chance!"

The ghosts swing low in the shimmering glow,
Painting the night with laughter in tow.
Secrets of the canopy, spun from delight,
In the dance of the shadows, they vanish from sight!

Uncharted Tales Beneath the Boughs

Deep in the woods where shadows play,
A squirrel's acorn takes flight today.
It spins on its tail, a dance so spry,
"Who stole my stash?" the owl asks the sky.

The mushrooms giggle, in colors bright,
As raccoons wear masks, much to their delight.
"Is that a hat?" a parrot squawks loud,
"Or just a leaf from last week's crowd?"

Beneath the boughs, the secrets twirl,
While butterflies chase leaves that swirl.
An echo of laughter through branches weave,
A treasure map drawn by a mischievous bee!

Now gather 'round, where secrets bloom,
Under the canopy, whispers loom.
Who knows the tales spun here so fine?
A fever of fun, in this playful shrine!

The Enduring Enigma

A shadow with stripes lumbers near,
Is it a cat or a lost souvenir?
With a wink and a pounce, it jumps back,
"Just visiting, mate, on my own quirky track!"

The ferns start to giggle, in rustling tones,
As whispers of squirrels rattle their bones.
"Why did the tree blush?" they hoot with glee,
"Because it saw the forest take a pee!"

From high up, a raven croaks, "What gives?"
"Nature's the stage, and we all are its kids!"
With each twist and turn, we snicker and laugh,
A maze of confusion, a colorful path.

So join in the fun, let your questions fly,
As wise old trees watch with a knowing eye.
Though answers may vanish like mist in the dawn,
The joy of the journey is never all gone!

Nature's Cryptogram

In the grove where the shadows loom,
A wise old cypress hums a tune.
"Scratch your head, oh human friend,
What's that shape? A bark or a bend?"

A ladybug giggles, dressed in red,
"Oops! Sorry, I tripped on a tree stump's head."
A raccoon nearby snickers in glee,
"Try guessing my riddle, and you'll see me free!"

Beneath thick vines, a mystery trails,
"Why did the chicken cross the snails?"
"Because they knew it was the longest way,
For a joke like that brightens the day!"

Amid the green, where laughter spills,
The trees conspire, they share their thrills.
In nature's code, with giggles and cheer,
Unlock the fun, for the answer is near!

The Echoing Enchantment

With each rustle of leaves, a joke takes flight,
The branches are buzzing with sheer delight.
"Why did the owl bring a suitcase today?
To finally escape the cat's dismay!"

In the crook of the trunk, two hedgehogs rhyme,
"Rolling in laughter might take some time.
What do you call a bear in disguise?
An 'Im-bear-d' who's clever and wise!"

Glimmers of sunlight, on petals they dance,
As trickling streams join in, taking a chance.
With every chuckle the forest knows,
It's the glee of the wild that wonderfully grows.

So come take a stroll, let the whimsies ignite,
In the laughter and joy, hearts feel so light.
For in echoes of mirth, we play hide and seek,
In the heart of the green, we're all cheek to cheek!

Reflections Among Roots

In a tangle of trunks, where whispers play,
Squirrels debate on the best nut to sway.
An acorn once claimed it was truly a king,
But a wise old crow only laughed at the thing.

A rabbit once tried to wear a twig hat,
And the flowers all giggled at the sight of that.
Toads croak their jokes, while the beetles all cheer,
Nature's own comedy, we're lucky to hear.

The roots share their stories in chuckles and snorts,
Of a snail that once traveled to gather smart thoughts.
But time, oh time, made him slow as a slug,
Now he's just a legend, wrapped up in a hug.

So when you stroll through the shady and bright,
Listen closely for laughter, a tickle of light.
For beneath every leaf, in each twist and turn,
The forest remembers, and it loves to return.

Secrets of the Shaded Realm

Under branches so wide, where the shadows nod,
A chipmunk wrote tales that made raindrops applaud.
In a dance-off with ferns, they twisted and spun,
Till the sun turned to amber, declaring them fun.

A wise old owl hooted, 'This time it's my turn,'
To tell all the secrets that the sunflowers yearn.
But the daisies all giggled, declaring their rule,
They spun a tall tale of a frog in a pool.

The bumblebees buzz with a quick little quip,
Of a leaf who once dreamed it could do a backflip.
But it flopped on a twig, no grace in its fall,
Yet laughter erupted; the best part of all!

So come join the merry in this leafy abyss,
Where the giggles of nature send sounds into bliss.
With each secret unraveled, we find something dear,
In the heart of the green, joy is always near.

The Gaze of the Oak

In the arms of the oak, where the shadows unite,
Sits a raccoon who claims, 'I'm the king of the night!'
But the fireflies wink, saying, 'That's quite the dream,'
They know he just steals from the garbage, it seems.

A woodpecker laughs at the tales he spins high,
Pecking at knots, he wonders why they don't fly.
The oak simply sways with an air of disdain,
While the winds hum a tune that drives critters insane.

Underneath the grand canopy, games are afoot,
A worm spreads the word that a beetle is cute.
But the beetle just scoffs, feeling quite quite aloof,
While the squirrel takes pictures to share with the roof.

So next time you wander beneath branches old,
Remember the stories, the laughter retold.
For in the oak's gaze, secrets and jokes thrive,
In this vibrant community, we all feel alive.

Adventures in Arboreal Shadows

In a sea of green, where the sun likes to peek,
A gopher in goggles called out, 'Look at me speak!'
He's trading his stories for seeds and for roots,
While ants hold a meeting in silly little suits.

A hedgehog in shades claimed he solved many a riddle,
But got lost in the branches and played a strange fiddle.
He serenaded the leaves with a tune made of rust,
And the laughter was wild—oh, how it combust!

The wind carried jokes from the pines to the oaks,
Where friendships flourish, and sharing's no hoax.
A turtle joined in, slow but with great flair,
Claiming 'I'll win by the time you all care!'

So gather together in this jolly green place,
Where the humor is plenty, none ever a waste.
For in shadows of giants, laughter's the key,
In the heart of these woods, let's all roam free.

Fables Between the Firs

In a grove where shadows play,
A squirrel hoards its acorn day.
It hides them here, it hides them there,
Why can't it find them? Oh, despair!

The owl winks with a knowing grin,
While the rabbit hops in a flurry of spin.
The creek gurgles with a chuckle or two,
Who left the violets to turn quite blue?

A fox in socks struts down the lane,
Wearing stripes that cause much disdain.
The bears giggle as they roll in the mud,
Who's got the best fashion? Oh, what a thud!

Underneath the laughing trees,
Pinecones drop with a gentle breeze.
A tale unfolds with every laugh,
Join us now for the woodland's craft!

The Soliloquy of Starlight

The moonlight dances on sleepy logs,
A cricket converses with bemused frogs.
"Why's the pond so full of dreams?"
"Perhaps," replies one, "life's not as it seems!"

The stars giggle, twinkling bright,
As fireflies flash with delight at night.
A raccoon juggles berries with glee,
"Don't drop them now!" yells a wise old bee.

The owls swoop in with theatrical flair,
"Why must the night be filled with air?"
A shadow rustles, a prankster's hide,
Who's in the tree? Come to decide!

The echo of laughter rolls from the hill,
"Why do we play this delightful thrill?"
Each rustle reveals mysterious joys,
In the starlight's magic, we're all just toys!

Whispers of the Windward Woods

In the trees where whispers creep,
The parrot tells jokes that make all leap.
"Why did the squirrel cross the road?"
To find the best stash, it's quite the load!

A deer prances with a giggle so sweet,
"What's with the moss that tickles my feet?"
The fox sings out, "Your style is neat,
But let's not get lost in this comic feat."

Branches sway, releasing their tales,
Of planters, dancers, and cheese that impales.
A clamor erupts from the wooden knolls,
"Who stole my snacks? Oh dear, it's trolls!"

As dusk draws near, the laughter swells,
Creatures unite in their zany spells.
With every breeze, they share the cheer,
In the woods, the funny things appear!

The Reverie of Rustling Leaves

Beneath the canopy where shadows twine,
A leaf giggled, "I'm just divine!"
"I dance with the wind, I skip and I sway,
Who knew a leaf could have such a play?"

A spider spun tales that tickled the air,
While the ants held a dance without a care.
"Do ants wear shoes?" asked a passing bee,
"Only when they're feeling fancy, you see!"

The hedgehog chimed in with a prickly cheer,
"I've rolled in the mud, and it's a good year!"
While the tree trunk chuckled, "What's that I hear?
Just a little laughter, well, bring it near!"

As the sun sets and the stars peek through,
The woods come alive with fun and skew.
Every rustle, every chuckle reveals,
Life's simple joys that the forest conceals!

The Riddle of the Rooted Realm

In a forest where shadows dance,
The squirrels wear tiny pants.
A whispering tree starts to chime,
Asking if it's breakfast time.

A gopher with a monocle frowns,
Counting acorns, wearing crowns.
He challenges all who pass by,
To find the nuts that are awry.

The chipmunks giggle, they seem to know,
What the wise old owl won't show.
They scurry here, they scurry there,
With leaves stuck up in their hair.

But none can solve the mystic quest,
Of who can find the acorn best.
A riddle wrapped in bark so tight,
In the realm where day meets night.

The Secrets of the Shimmering Glade

In the glade where fairies scheme,
A toad sings out a silly dream.
With sparkles 'round and laughter bright,
They throw a party each moonlight.

The fireflies flash like bulbs of glee,
Dancing 'round a spilled cup of tea.
One brave spider spins a tune,
While gossiping with a friendly moon.

A joke about a lost shoe floats,
Carried by the tiniest gnomes' boats.
They paddle past in a giggly race,
With splashes that burst in silly pace.

If you can catch a bubble's gleam,
You'll uncover the glade's best theme.
A secret shared among the leaves,
Is laughter, oh, what joy it weaves!

Allure in the Ancient Leaves

In the rustle of the ancient trees,
A raccoon reads the latest tease.
It's all about a tree stump's flair,
With vines that tickle without care.

"Why don't trees like to play cards?"
A wise old crow asks from the yards.
"Because they might get stumped for sure,
And lose their bark in the allure!"

The squirrels chuckle, they know the trick,
To draw a smile with a little flick.
They play hide-and-seek in a fashion rare,
Behind the trunks, scampering without a care.

Amidst the whispers of the breeze,
Join the laughter 'neath the trees.
The ancient leaves laugh loud and free,
With riddles whispered in glee.

The Veil of Venerable Trees

In the shadow where giants loom,
A hedgehog hums a silly tune.
Lurking 'neath the verdant veil,
A secret waits, a wondrous tale.

The branches twist in playful jest,
As bees compete in a buzzing quest.
"Who can find the sweetest flower?"
The daisies giggle, feeling power.

The wise old trunk, adorned with moss,
Winks at critters, bearing no loss.
A riddle lingers in the air,
With silly puns, it's quite a flair.

"Why was the tree so good at math?"
It counted rings with a leafy path.
When laughter rules the ancient woods,
You'll find the joy in nature's goods.

Tales of the Timeless Timber

In a forest of giants, a squirrel named Dave,
Found a nut that he thought would be quite the rave.
He slathered it with honey, a sticky delight,
But forgot it was lunch and he ate it by night.

A wise old owl perched high in a tree,
Shared stories of acorns, and laughter, you see.
With each little tale, the critters would cheer,
Until all were giggling, and forgot all their fear.

A raccoon in shades claimed he was the king,
While the chipmunks just danced and began to sing.
They fashioned a crown from some fallen leaves,
And decided that laughter serves best in their eves.

So if you wander where the tall redwoods sway,
Catch wind of their antics and join in the play.
For in this grand grove, the jokes never end,
With each twist of the trunk, there's more fun to send.

Ponderings in the Pines

Beneath the tall pines, a squirrel's first thought,
Is why do the branches sway if they're not caught?
He decided to ask with a whisker-twitch shake,
But the response he got was a giggle, not fake.

A porcupine pondered, with quills all a-prick,
If a tree falls alone, does it make sound or stick?
He jotted it down on a leaf made of ink,
Then tripped on a root and fell in the drink.

A chorus of critters were laughing so bright,
As the porcupine splashed and took flight in mid-flight.
They welcomed him back, with a hug and a grin,
And taught him the ways of the giggle within.

So if you ponder in the tall wooded scene,
Remember to laugh, it's the best kind of green.
For thoughts may tumble like pinecones someday,
But laughter will catch them and carry away.

The Quest of the Quaking Aspen

A brave little aspen, named Tim, took a dare,
To find the best joke while dancing in air.
With leaves that would tremble, he searched with delight,

For giggles and chuckles to share every night.

He met a wise fox who told him this riddle:
What bounces with joy yet isn't that fragile?
Tim scratched his bark and thought very hard,
Then spun like a whirlwind, and answered, 'My yard!'

With a grin stretched wide, the fox laughed with glee,
And they danced through the glen, just as wild as could be.
They tumbled and rolled, creating a mess,
But each little stumble led to more happiness.

So if you seek laughter in the forest divine,
Look for the aspen, who's ever so fine.
He'll spin you a tale, and the joy will take flight,
With laughter like leaves in the warm summer night.

The Elusive Echo of the Elders

In the shadow of giants, the echoes would call,
A parrot named Pete thought he could mimic them all.
He squawked and he squawked, but missed every cue,
Instead, he just sounded like a boat full of stew.

The old maple chuckled, its leaves swaying high,
'Keep trying, dear Pete, someday you'll touch the sky!'
With determination, the bird flapped and danced,
And turned every blunder into joy, enhanced.

Soon critters gathered, their sides split with glee,
As the parrot kept trying, just wanting to be.
The echoes returned with a giggle, not fright,
For laughter bounced back in the soft evening light.

So if ever you wander where the whispers confide,
Join in on the fun, and let cheer be your guide.
For even the echoes from elders you'll find,
Are full of a magic that's both sweet and kind.

Mysteries of the Tallest Trees

In the forest so high, what do we see?
The squirrels debate, sipping herbal tea.
They argue and jest, what's the best nut?
One says it's acorns, the other says 'shut!'

The trunks wear their scars like medals of pride,
With whispers of secrets, they stand side by side.
They giggle at stumps, who moan and complain,
'We had our day, now we're just plain!'

A woodpecker knocks with a tap-tap-tap,
What's hidden above? The shy owl nap!
He peeks from his perch, gives a sleepy yawn,
"Why do you bother? Sleep till the dawn!"

The branches dance low, the sun rays peek,
As shadows play tricks, the mischief they seek.
Catch a glimpse of the joy, in this towering spree,
The tallest trees cherish their comedy!

Enigmas of the Ancient Grove

In the grove so old, where the whispers reside,
A fox tells his tales with a cheeky glide.
He spins out a joke, but no one quite gets,
What's a tree without leaves? A trunk full of regrets!

The owls hoot loudly, discussing their flight,
Who aims for the best branch—what a silly sight!
"Last night's mouse!" one claims with a wink and a grin,
"Fluffier than clouds, but better tasting?"

The vines like to giggle, in tangled embrace,
They tickle the squirrels, who engage in a race.
"To climb is to conquer!" they shout with delight,
But trip on their tails, oh what a sight!

As shadows play games, in the dappled bright,
The secrets of trees come out in the light.
What's the wisest old sage now taking a nap?
Why the ancient oak, who's found a warm gap!

Shadows in the Sunlight

In the sunlight's glow, shadows dance and tease,
They stretch and they twist with the afternoon breeze.
A rabbit hops by, with a tip of his hat,
"Why are you all jumping? Are you doing acrobat?"

Leaves whisper stories, rustling with glee,
As bugs join the party, a bustling spree.
One fly buzzes loudly, thinking he's grand,
"I'm the best of the party, come take my hand!"

The sunbeams chuckle, tickling the ground,
While ants march in line, making soft sounds.
"Why carry the crumbs?" one tiny ant said,
"There's plenty of food in our cozy bed!"

With giggles all around in their noisy retreat,
Shadows and sunlight make life so sweet.
Every day is a riddle, filled with such cheer,
In the funny old grove, where laughter is near!

The Language of Leaves

Under emerald crowns, the leaves softly speak,
With whispers and chuckles, their language unique.
A leaf puffed with pride says, "I'm quite the catch,
I caught the best breeze, but I didn't scratch!"

The other leaves sigh with a fluttering laugh,
"Have you seen our friend? He's a tall, leafy staff!"
"He's got all the gossip from trees to the ground,
Ask him about Mr. Acorn! Quite profound!"

The winds carry tales, they twist and they twirl,
Of blossoms and buzzing in a bright, fragrant whirl.
"Why don't you join us?" the petals would jive,
"We'll show you the way to feel truly alive!"

In this canopy world, life's funny and bright,
With laughter as currency, come bask in the light.
The language of leaves, so sweet it would seem,
Is a comedy show in a woodland dream!

Nature's Cryptic Tale

In the forest deep and wide,
Trees with secrets still abide.
The squirrels chatter, laugh and play,
Whispering hints of a curious day.

Mossy rocks with smiles peek,
Echoing time in a game of sneak.
Branches wave like silly hosts,
Inviting all to join their roasts.

The owls hoot with glee at night,
Quizzing stars in their glowing light.
Nature's jesters, wild and free,
Set the stage for glee's decree.

So wander here and try to guess,
What the wind brings, a playful mess.
With every step, a chuckle waits,
In this green maze, joy elates.

A Question of Roots

Underneath the towering trees,
Lies a puzzle solved with ease.
Roots entwined like a prankster's joke,
Whispering tales that twist and poke.

The ferns flap as if to cheer,
While raccoons scurry, drawing near.
"Who's the king of this green spread?"
They ask while munching, half out of dread.

"Is it the worm or the sneaky snail?
Or perhaps the lizard with a tiny tail?"
Each critter giggles, eyes wide and bright,
As they ponder their roles in the moonlight.

So dig a little, laugh a lot,
Nature's humor is quite the plot.
With every turn, a mystery blooms,
Amidst the gnarled roots and leafy rooms.

Veils of Fog and Fable

The fog rolls in like a cheeky sprite,
Playing tricks with morning light.
Shadows dance and giggle soft,
As laughter echoes from the loft.

Through the mist, a fuzzy shape,
Maybe a fox, or a wise escape.
With a wink, it darts away,
Leaving us guessing, come what may.

"Is it a thief or a friend so bold?
Maybe it's just a tale retold?"
The trees whisper with a painted grin,
As the fog teases, drawing us in.

So let's embrace the morning haze,
Where stories tumble in playful ways.
In the whispers of the tangled wood,
Fun awaits, misunderstood!

The Silent Storyteller

A grand old tree stands proud and tall,
Its bark etched with time's scrawl.
With branches thick, it holds a quirk,
Of tales and fables, a hidden perk.

"Gather 'round," it seems to say,
"You've come on a most curious day!"
As birds croon with a chuckle and trill,
They spin yarns that bring us a thrill.

The wise old owl gives a nod,
As picnicking folks trot and plod.
With each bite of sandwich, a giggle flows,
From the laughter that the forest knows.

So pause a moment, inhale the glee,
Nature's humor is wild and free.
With every sigh under leafy embrace,
Find the joy in this magical space.

Laughter in the Leaves

A squirrel in a tie, so dapper and spry,
Juggles acorns and laughs, oh my, oh my!
The chipmunks join in, a dance they can't hide,
While the trees shake their branches, they giggle with pride.

The owl hoots a riddle, quite wise and absurd,
"What has feathers but isn't a bird?"
The answer comes quick, with a burst of delight,
It's a ticklish tickle from a tree's furry height.

A fox tells a tale of a lost little shoe,
He chuckles so hard, he joins in the crew.
The woods echo laughter, a symphonic cheer,
As creatures unite, spreading joy far and near.

At dusk, they all gather, a jolly old bunch,
With stories and snacks, they share a nice lunch.
The moon tunes in, with a grin on its face,
In the playful embrace of this whimsical space.

The Enigma of the Elderwoods

A tree with a grin, its bark full of laughs,
Whispers wisecracks between each tree's drafts.
A woodpecker knocks, joins in with the jest,
What a curious place for a comedy fest!

The fog rolls in thick, like a woolly old sock,
"Why did the tree stop? It couldn't find its clock!"
The pine trees chuckle, their needles a-twitch,
While shadows dance jiggles without a hitch.

A beetle in boots prances round on the floor,
"Excuse me, my friends, I hear knocking at the door!"
It's a snail with a smile, carrying cake,
The woods sing in glee, for the fun they all make.

As sunset approaches, the laughter grows loud,
With every wisecrack, they gather a crowd.
So lift up your spirits, let merriment flow,
In the kingdom of giants, where giggles do grow.

Beneath the Boughs

Beneath the thick branches, the fun never ends,
Where mushrooms tell jokes, and laughter transcends.
A rabbit in sneakers does flips by the creek,
While a frog cracks a laugh, quite unusual and cheeky.

The wind sings a tune, a diddy of cheer,
But what's even funnier, it doesn't have ears!
A family of raccoons debates with their paws,
"Why did the leaf fall? It's got no laws!"

The elder tree chuckles, its leaves all aglow,
"Why don't scientists trust? Because they just don't know!"
The critters all snicker, what a riotous sound,
In this funny forest, where giggles abound.

As twilight descends, the fireflies sway,
Dancing in rhythm, a bright cabaret.
So come share a laugh, join in on the spree,
For under these boughs, it's a wild jubilee.

Codes from the Old Growth

Two owls and a beaver plot mischief with pride,
Decoding the secrets that in shadows abide.
"Why did the branch break? It didn't keep fit!"
The crack of a chuckle makes their laughter emit.

The hedgehog pops in, with a riddle so neat,
"What's round and will roll, but doesn't have feet?"
The answer comes quick, like a bolt from on high,
"A donut!" they shout, as they all start to cry.

A playful old badger draws dots in the dirt,
"Here's a mystery, what wears a green shirt?"
The clan starts to ponder, while buzzing like bees,
Could it be the grass? Or perhaps it's the trees?

With giggles and snorts, they find the last clue,
Wrapped inside laughter — a wonderful view.
So gather your friends in this forest so grand,
Where the codes and the chuckles go hand in hand.

Syllables of the Sequoias

Tall trees whisper, secrets play,
Squirrels giggle, darting away.
A branch that creaks, a trunk that grins,
Who knew a bark could lead to wins?

Silly shadows dance and sway,
Mossy carpets where fairies lay.
The roots tickle, though feet are low,
In wild woods, laughter starts to grow.

A bird with shades of purple hue,
Says, "Guess my name, I'll play with you!"
With every chirp, a teasing peek,
In this forest, it's fun to sneak!

So as we wander, let's not frown,
Nature's jesters wear the crown.
With each surprise, a grin we'll show,
In the grove where the fun winds blow.

Whims of the Wilderness

In the woods where the wild things cheer,
A babbling brook brings chuckles near.
A raccoon's mask, so sly and funny,
Swapping tales for scraps and honey.

A signpost points to nowhere fast,
"Turn left for squirrels, right for the past!"
Trees giggle, swaying left and right,
Playing games till the fall of night.

A woodpecker drumming a silly song,
Proclaims, "Nature's here! You can't go wrong!"
With every tap, the trees respond,
Making music that goes beyond.

Amongst the leaves, a rabbit leaps,
With wise old owls, who share their peeps.
In this place where wild whims unfurl,
Every twist and turn is a playful whirl.

The Puzzle of the Pines

Pine cones scatter, a playful jest,
What's hidden here? A curious quest.
A yappy fox with a tale to share,
Says riddles bloom in the forest air.

Tall sentinels wear their hats with pride,
Whispering secrets in the breeze outside.
"Find the acorn that rolls in glee,
It holds a fortune, come and see!"

Mushrooms giggle as they change their hats,
Little hedgehogs plot and share small chats.
"Who's gainfully employed in this corner of green?
Maybe the toad or the grass so keen?"

The forest guards its quirks so bold,
With every heartbeat, a story told.
In shadows deep, laughter hides tight,
Join the throng of woodland delight!

Unraveling the Forest's Secrets

Bamboo tickles with a gentle swish,
Who knew whispers could grant a wish?
Boughs are stretching, allowing mirth,
As woodlands spin secrets of the earth.

A grinning bear plays hide and seek,
While ants choreograph a tiny sneak.
Who can guess the route of the breeze?
With swirls and twirls that tease with ease!

The owls hoot riddles into the night,
Taxing logic in soft moonlight.
Between the ferns, the laughs will leap,
Nature's puzzle, forever deep.

So come and roam where the fun's alive,
In the tangled woods where stories thrive.
With every step, let laughter grow,
In the heart of the wild, let your spirit flow.

Shadows Hiding in Tall Trees

In the branches where squirrels play,
A secret dance in the light of day.
What has wings but does not fly?
A leaf that waves as the breezes sigh.

Beneath the shade, where whispers roam,
What sits still but calls you home?
A shadow chats with a fuzzy bee,
But what's the buzz? It's all a spree!

Gnomes chuckle as they sip their tea,
What's always there but you cannot see?
A laugh on the breeze, a wink from the bark,
Underneath the stars, it's quite the lark!

Amongst the giants, where secrets bloom,
What wears a crown yet gives no room?
A mushroom peers with a curious face,
In the tall trees, we frolic and chase.

Puzzles of the Timeless Forest

Beneath the canopy, the laughter flows,
What starts with 'T' and ends with 'O's?
A tiptoe of creatures, all in a line,
Each doing their best to seem quite fine.

Fungi giggle as they spread their cheer,
What can you hold but cannot steer?
The sunlight dances on blades of grass,
While shadows hold secrets in a playful mass.

The trees stand tall, with a curious grin,
Who came to visit, but never goes in?
A breeze that tickles the top of your nose,
In the forest's charm, where the laughter grows.

By the old oak, what whispers low?
An echo of fun, putting on a show!
With every giggle, the tall trees sway,
As they tell the tales of a gleeful day.

The Oak's Silent Query

In the quiet shade where owls blink,
What can you sip but never drink?
The morning dew on a sunflower bright,
Brings smiles to faces, oh what a sight!

The oak stands wise with branches so wide,
What has a spine but cannot hide?
A riddle etched on the bark so old,
Tales of mischief and laughter untold.

The winds carry whispers of days gone by,
What takes the road but doesn't reply?
A clumsy squirrel with acorn in hand,
Creates clattering giggles, a merry band.

Under the leaves, an adventure awaits,
What rolls through life but never dissipates?
The giggles of nature in perfect array,
In the light of the morning, we frolic and play.

Conundrums in the Arboreal Realm

In the woods where the shadows leap,
What has a mouth but cannot speak?
A brook that babbles with stories of old,
With every ripple, its secrets unfold.

Among the trunks, a puzzle to share,
What can you catch but does not snare?
The flutter of butterflies, so free and spry,
Dancing on air as the breezes sigh.

The forest laughs as the critters conspire,
What's often mistaken for something higher?
A mound of leaves that forms a soft bed,
Where sleepy heads rest and dreams can be fed.

Under the cover of a starry night,
What ties up the trees but feels so light?
A blanket of stars sprinkled with glee,
In the arboreal realm, it's a jubilee!

www.ingramcontent.com/pod-product-compliance
Lightning Source LLC
Chambersburg PA
CBHW071822160426
43209CB00003B/167